Martin Murphy

Victim

D1513026

Bloomsbury Methuen Drama
An imprint of Bloomsbury Publishing Plc

B L O O M S B U R Y

LONDON · OXFORD · NEW YORK · NEW DELHI · SYDNEY

Bloomsbury Methuen Drama

An imprint of Bloomsbury Publishing Plc

Imprint previously known as Methuen Drama

50 Bedford Square	1385 Broadway
London	New York
WC1B 3DP	NY 10018
UK	USA

www.bloomsbury.com

BLOOMSBURY, METHUEN DRAMA and the Diana logo
are trademarks of Bloomsbury Publishing Plc

First published 2017

© Martin Murphy, 2017

British Library Cataloguing-in-Publication Data

A catalogue record for this book is available from the British Library.

ISBN: PB: 978-1-3500-5807-1
e-PDF: 978-1-3500-5808-8
ePub: 978-1-3500-5809-5

Library of Congress Cataloging in Publication Data

A catalog record for this book is available from the Library of Congress

Series: Modern Plays

Cover design: Olivia D'Cruz
Cover image © Bruised Sky Productions

Typeset by Country Setting, Kingsdown, Kent CT14 8ES
Printed and bound in Great Britain

To find out more about our authors and books visit www.bloomsbury.com.
Here you will find extracts, author interviews, details of forthcoming events
and the option to sign up for our newsletters.

Bruised Sky Productions
present

VICTIM

by Martin Murphy

Victim

previewed at Old Red Lion Theatre, London,
on 28 July 2017, before opening at The Attic,
Pleasance Courtyard, Edinburgh, on 2 August.

Presented by Bruised Sky Productions Ltd

The cast was as follows:

Tracey / Siobhan	Louise Beresford
Director	Martin Murphy
Sound and Lighting Designer	Kevin Millband
Operator	Amée Smith

Creative Team

Writer/Director | Martin Murphy

Martin was appointed Artistic Director of Bruised Sky Productions in 2017.
His recent plays include *Worlds* (VAULT Festival, 2017), *RockStar* (Lyric
Hammersmith, YHWF 2017) and *Villain* (Underbelly, Edinburgh, 2016).
His previous works for stage include *Manor* (Soho Theatre) and *Barren*
(24 Hour Plays, Old Vic Theatre).

As a performer Martin is half of the musical comedy double act Pistol
and Jack, who have performed at a large number of venues including
Secret Garden Party, Assembly Edinburgh, Nu:Write Festival Zagreb and
Soho Theatre.

Performer | Louise Beresford

Louise trained at Mountview Academy. Her theatre credits include Lady
Macbeth in *Macbeth in Pitch Black* with the London Theatre Company (St
James Theatre), Goneril in *King Lear* with Lazarus Theatre Company (The
Space), Julia in *The Crazy Locomotive* (The Cockpit), Laura Lee in *Battle Lines*
for Raising Dark Theatre Company (Finborough) and Berthe Morisot in
Madame Manet for Rough Haired Pointer (Tabard Theatre). Louise has
appeared in comedy shows at Leicester Square Theatre, Theatre503 and
Soho Theatre and is part of comedy group Lead Pencil, who have appeared
on BBC Radio 4 and Comedy Central.

Lighting and Sound Designer | Kevin Millband

Kevin is the Technical Manager of Bruised Sky Productions. He trained in
Literature and Imaginative Writing and has since worked as a technician and
sound and lighting designer in venues across London and at the Edinburgh
Fringe Festival. Kevin is also Production Manager of the award-winning
Crafternoon Cabaret Club.

Operator | Amée Smith

Amée is an actor, stage manager and producer who trained at Rose Bruford
in the UK, Stephen F Austin in Texas and Centre College, Kentucky, in the
USA. Working across theatre and comedy in immersive and traditional
formats, Amée has recently worked with Amused Moose Comedy, London
Clown Festival, Hornsey Town Hall Arts Centre for the Crouch End Festival,
Clown Fest Manchester, Honky-Bonk Theatre, The Establishment and
Flabbergast Theatre in London and Edinburgh.

Associate Producer | Hannah Cox

Hannah is Young People's Programme Manager at the National Theatre and has been working in Arts Education for twelve years. She has extensive experience in programming and producing for Southbank Centre, Soho Theatre and numerous smaller organisations, as well as running her own company, Crafternoon Cabaret Club. Hannah is a passionate advocate for political theatre and new writing.

Associate Producer | Alan Stratford

Alan began his career in Norwich, directing *The Resistible Rise of Arturo Ui* at the Garage Theatre and creating *Freshers* at the UEA Drama Studio. He went on to facilitate the National Theatre's New Views scheme at the EM Forster Theatre, Tonbridge School, and has been Literary Coordinator at the King's Head Theatre in Islington. He has also worked across a number of roles at Regent's Park Open Air Theatre, Little Angel Theatre, Hope Theatre and Soho Theatre. When not working or seeing shows, Alan is likely to be supporting his football team, Wolverhampton Wanderers.

Associate Artist| Jules Haworth

Jules is Education Producer at Soho Theatre and runs the Writers' Lab and Comedy Lab programmes for emerging artists. Dramaturgy credits include *Brute* by Izzy Tennyson (Ideas Tap Underbelly Award, 2015), *Muscovado* by Matilda Ibini (Alfred Fagon Award, 2015), *In Your Image* by Gemma Copping (Soho Theatre Young Writers' Award, 2013), *On the Edge of Me* by Yolanda *Mercy* (tour) and *The Dogs of War* by Tim Foley (Old Red Lion). Jules' play *Pigeon Steps* was longlisted for the Adrian Pagan Award, 2014.

Founder | James Kermack

James founded Bruised Sky Productions in 2009 and was the company's first Artistic Director. He wrote and directed the critically acclaimed five-star play *Lads* before directing Martin Murphy's play *Manor*. James has also directed over forty theatre productions as a freelance director before moving into film and television.

His debut feature film *Hi-Lo Joe*, completed in 2015, was chosen to be a part of Film London Breakthrough playing at the BFI Southbank in 2016 and had its world premiere at the prestigious 27th Dinard British Film Festival, where James was also a jury member. His second feature, multi-million-pound action thriller *Knuckledust*, shoots across three countries in 2017. In September 2016 he was announced as Head of Creative Development at Featuristic Films.

Bruised Sky Productions

Bruised Sky Productions was founded by James Kermack in 2009 with the current Artistic Director Martin Murphy joining later that year. The company's first production, *Lads*, received a range of five- and four-star reviews at the Edinburgh Fringe Festival before a London run at the Canal Cafe.

Bruised Sky most recently presented *Worlds* at VAULT Festival in January 2017, following the success of *Villain* at the Edinburgh Fringe Festival, 2016, and its subsequent London transfer to the King's Head Theatre.

Bruised Sky's other works include *Manor* by Martin Murphy, which played at Soho Theatre before a three-week run at Tristan Bates Theatre, Covent Garden, and *Animal Bordello* by David Scinto, writer of the Oscar-nominated classic *Sexy Beast*.

Special thanks to

Chris Hawitt, Georgia Sykes, Carol Murphy, Alan Stratford, Brian Murphy, Hannah Cox, Rosie Smith, Julia Murray, Trevor Murphy, Maddie Rice, Daniel Goldman, Becci Gemmell and all the people who gave individually or via our Indiegogo campaign and made this production possible.

Victim

Characters

Tracey, *a prison officer*
Siobhan, *a prisoner*

Setting

England

Time

The present

Author's Note

Although locations are occasionally described in the text, in no way is it my intention for the set to accurately recreate these. The play favours a non-naturalistic staging, although this is obviously at the discretion of individual directors.

Punctuation and spelling are used to indicate delivery, not to conform to the rules of grammar.

Scene One

Tracey   This is how it starts. You show the slightest, kindness. You give half a bloody . . . Less than that, you give a thousandth of an inch they won't just take a mile. You're done. Whole thing's gone. This girl's asked me to bring in a phone, friendly, but also kind of begging, says she just wants to check on her daughter, her little girl's not well and she wants to check on her. I don't even engage, make eye contact, just walk away and she tries to stay friendly begging like then snaps, 'You're a fucking bitch Tracey,' she shouts at me and all sorts, I've checked out. It is bloody crazy what people will do to get phones in this place. Try to play games, mental battles; I love battles, give me one with anyone I'll win it.

George, one of the other officers, he talks, mostly what he talks is how long he's been in this place, same jokes, same jokes over and again, he can be funny though. He's been in prisons twenty years, twelve years when he was living up near Rugby, then eight down here. Phone-wise he's got a hundred stories he says, but he just seems to tell three of them, over and over again. (*As George.*) 'So he's stripped and I've got the gloves on and I say, look fella before we do this is there anything up there I'm gonna find cos if there is it'd be nicer for us both if you just fish it out yourself. And the lad goes, no, nothing you'll find on me. So I has to check and I look up and it's like Aladdin's cave up there, it's like a shopping centre car park on a Saturday afternoon, it's rammed. And up there, baccy and what have you, but after that, there's a mobile phone and *two* mobile phone chargers, the prongs on 'em can you imagine? So I've asked him, not just annoyed he's lied to me and made me fish all that out, but now I'm intrigued so I says, lad why two? And he's, well one's for the iPhone for me but my mate he don't trust Apple, reckons they're taking over the world so that's for his Samsung.'

That's the lengths they'll go to, to get phones in here, well not just phones anything, and they'll look for the weak, you show the slightest sign that you're friendly, care, vulnerable. But I don't engage. I don't make mistakes and today, well today I'm super bloody unengaged in them, because today our special guest arrives, it's March 25th. Followed the trial. Her identity protected from the media but in here, well there's no place to hide in here. I never follow court cases but this one, you couldn't avoid it for some reason, every headline and once she was sentenced, well it weren't like there was that big a range of places she could end up in, not a foreign dignitary booking a stay in the Ritz. No she'll be in here and I know what I said, I don't get involved but as a human I do, I wanna meet her.

Scene Two

Siobhan   You want to ask. You want to ask don't you? 'What you done to be in 'ere Siobhan?' Well I'll tell ya from the middle, cos the beginning? Well I don't know where the beginning'd be. I'm staying in Liverpool at the time, I don't know why. I've got this CD in my hand and I walk into this bar just next to Lime Street, it's four o'clock in afternoon but I'm buzzing and I give 'em the CD.

Music plays.

And it's Ibiza hits 2008 from the year I was working there, nineteen, dancing. I wasn't paid to dance, my job was to get people on a night out into our bar, I was a PR, like a rep, but I was dancing, dancing all summer, that's all I remember doing. And I've got 'em to put the CD on and I'm dancing in there and there's just a few of the cabbies in there and one fella has actually got a book, like to read. He stands out a mile as he's the only one not looking at me. And I'm dancing, and while I'm dancing I decide. Talk premeditated I guess it was yeah, cos I decide and I get on the train, head Euston then from there I walk, walk the whole way to my ex's place and I've stabbed him. I've stabbed him full in the chest right there.

There was a girl there, that's not why I did it. She seemed alright. By alright I mean brutally horrified but she seemed like a nice person. She kept repeating herself about how they were set to go on holiday. Crete, they were flying to, the next day. She'd been looking forward to it. Seemed more upset about that really, considering she'd come to the door and found I'd stabbed her fella. It's hard I guess, we all need something to look forward to and once that's taken away. Well once that's taken away there's nothing left is there? Crete. I've been there years back, from the plane looking down on it, sunny, hot as fuck but from up there could see these dark black patches. You have to be above the clouds to see how dark a shadow they cast.

Stabbing him? I mean I had my reasons for doing it but that was before, like before the middle so . . . And how I ended up in the same cell as her, our most famous inmate. A23174? Well that's after the middle so.

Scene Three

Tracey   He's actually done something, booked us something. It's our five-year wedding anniversary and Terry has not just remembered, he's made plans, like not plans on the day like I can tell he's given this some thought, listened to things I've been talking about, I do drop some fairly big hints, well you have to, but he's picked up on them and he's acted. He wakes me up, well I wake up and he's out the room so I'm angry for just a sec thinking he's forgotten but then he's through and he's made breakfast in bed and a little bottle of fizz and we have a glass each and some croissants and he gives me a card and he's booked this show, he's remembered this show I've been talking about and that's how I know he must have got tickets quite a while back cos it's been sold out for months and he's found this lush-looking restaurant that we'll be going to before and I'm just really chuffed with what he's done and we have sex and we both enjoy it, at the same time. And it's just for the sake of enjoying it.

So we go for this meal and the food is awesome and the wine is, well we both like a wine anyway and we have two bottles which we're finishing and it means we've pushed it a bit for time but should be fine, should be just fine but now we can't . . . We can't get the waiter's attention, can't get our waiter's attention so we're making that gesture – (*Indicates the bill.*) But nobody is catching our eye until suddenly he does, our waiter sees me and he holds a finger to say 'One minute' and I relax but one minute passes then three and now we really are cutting it fine and I Google the show and it says there's no latecomers and I tell Terry there's no latecomers and he goes up to the counter bit with his card, but they just say, 'We'll bring it over' and smile but we will now miss the show if we don't so we have to, we're not doing a runner but we leave the restaurant without paying. And I'm just thinking, I cannot end up in prison, they tell you, 'Don't end up in here, it's so much worse for your lot on the inside,' and I've made a plan that if it comes to it that Terry takes the rap for us, just in my mind I've planned this then we're at the theatre and the usher is about to close the door but looks nervously at us and waving us in hurriedly. And Terry asks them where the loo is but they say 'It's starting now and latecomers aren't admitted,' and we've sat down in the theatre and it starts.

So the show starts and it's great but what I'm watching, from about five minutes in I'm watching Terry, shuffle and cross and uncross his legs then he grabs, I'm not sure what he's grabbing but he grabs what I now see is a plastic pint glass which was under seat next to his and he's taking off his shoe, and he's taking off his sock. And he puts the sock in the pint glass and now I know what he's going to do but it's too late, he's pissing, he's pissing in this pint pot and he's put the sock in there so it won't make a noise and I'm thinking yeah, yeah if one of us is going down for the restaurant thing it can be you.

Scene Four

Siobhan   This officer, Tracey. She loves asking me stuff, about what I got up to. Not crimes and that, just things I'd do, like on a night out. Back in Wicklow, Liverpool, London. It seems to just, I don't know if it cheers her up but . . . Well she likes hearing it and I don't mind telling. I don't think her husband loves her, well he might do but there's a problem there. Like I can see she's unhappy and I'm the one serving life in prison. But she'll always come find me and ask and so I tell her.

I'm on a night out and we've been partying all weekend, this is a Sunday now and I'm in this club-like bar place and I'm stood outside the toilets waiting, a bit fucked, and this lad comes out and he says, 'Are you waiting for someone?' and I look at him and he's alright and I say, 'You?' And suddenly our faces are heading into each other like a sex car crash, and his tongue's down my throat, and it's good. There is just a connection between us and it's electric. Everything just fits right and he's dragging me into the cubicles and he's inside me with his tongue and this is straight away better than the pills I've been doing all weekend or maybe they're just adding to this but this is immense, then he stands up and I'm returning the favour and I'm looking up at him and his eyeballs are rolling into the back of his head like he's possessed and he pulls me up and moves in me and we just fit, we just, connect and there's none of that usual stuff you have in club loos where you can't get your legs in the right place, this is like magic and we're done and he looks in my eyes and I'm pretty much sober by this point, like this has got my head back straight and I kiss him, not like the mad animal stuff we'd just been doing. My eyes meet his and I kiss him and I go.

Most of that's true from what I remember, I've maybe merged or . . . Stuff's always better in the past anyway isn't it but . . . ? The important thing is she thinks I'm everything she'd wanna be and I've made her current life seem like a pile of shit. There's a weakness there. This one is opening up and they're the ones you can use. I can get her drip, drip, drip. It'll take time, but I've got all the time in the world.

Scene Five

Tracey   We're not *not* trying. I know that sounds weird. It's just the sort of question people feel they can ask you if you're married, isn't it? 'Any kids? Are you trying or . . . ?' It's just not happened. I'd like it to, I think I'd . . . I do want us to. We were just using condoms then when we got serious I went on the pill but Terry said it made me '*more* mental', yeah. So I came off that and we went back to condoms then sometimes he just wouldn't bother then after we were married we just never bothered. It wasn't something we discussed, it wasn't a plan but I guess in a way it was, in a way. Because we stopped using them but then . . . Well, we barely do it now, so rarely do it but . . . I've had friends say have you thought about getting help with it? Seeing a doctor, finding out if one of you's . . . ? But no, thank you we'll just, as we are thank you. Things happen in their own time don't they? Don't they? But I would really like one.

We're planning my thirtieth and I'm dreading it, not getting old, I'm fine with the age, it's the questions, the fact that people assume they can ask you that. About babies and that look of . . . sympathy if you say it just hasn't happened yet, like they're so sorry for you. You're someone something bad has happened to, I hate that. I'm on the sofa and Terry asks me about it, my thirtieth not kids. He's still talking but I'm reading about that case again. Our new guest. I couldn't understand it, her, her own child and I Googled it, lots, but the thing was, the thing was that nobody really knew what had happened, like who'd actually done anything. She'd been with someone, a man, and he'd been, religious, in a way I guess. If you can call that sort of thing religion but he'd gone, nobody knew where he was so she . . . She was the only one could be charged and she just said, 'He was trying to cut the badness

out, it's gone from her now, she's pure now.' And that just
sounds so, horrible, mental but . . . But I spend hours each day,
I'm going to spend years with this woman but when I look in
her eyes I can see she believes that, even now trusts that. That
what she let happen to that baby, that he was just removing the
wrong. Like a surgeon cutting out a tumour. I don't hate this
woman. I'm going to help this woman.

'If we booked that room up at the top from early evening still
gets the light I reckon then could have balloons and stuff,
I could sort that. What you reckon?' says Terry. Yeah maybe,
I say. Terry tries to kiss me but I keep reading. Looking
forward to being back in work in a weird way. Next day.

Even from across the room, I'm not close but I can see she's
not really eating. Marcia. They try that stuff some of them, get
attention. But that don't seem like her, this ain't a plan.

I think it's now fair to say she's the object of my obsession.
There's a bit of me wonders if this is just to give myself
something to think about but I know there's an answer in here
somewhere. I don't know what it is yet obviously but like a quiz
question, you think about it for a while, plant the seed, then
just when you've moved two questions on the answer hits you.

I move over to her, 'Why you not eating?' She just smiles at me,
looks at my belt, doesn't speak. 'Is someone . . . ?' Again she
just smiles and doesn't say anything. I wanna get angry or,
make her answer me but . . . Well it's her food, she don't
wanna eat it she's gonna be hungry. Long wait till next meal.
The Irish one's hanging back, looking over like she wants to
talk, I don't meet her eye. My shift's done, locker, check my
phone, nineteen missed calls and texts from my sister, Dad's
had a heart attack.

Scene Six

Siobhan   So how we ended up in the same cell? Prisoner A23174, baby killer? We can't tell you her real name. You know who she is. It's stupid but . . . We're not allowed to tell you. Here. I think in the media they called her Marcia, so we'll call her that too. She's smiling, but not happy-smiling, she's scared and she's showing she's scared. You don't show you're scared.

First day she arrived, I watched, that's what I do, I learn. I watch the guard Tracey, she just stares at her, 'You know who that is? She'll die in here.' I says to her, not a threat I'm making, just an observation. She makes it her business to talk to Marcia that day, like she's looking for something. Evil? Guilt? I just see emptiness if anything but I can see in Tracey there's an opening here.

Being the person in here everyone wants to come to makes you realise, the main thing people want in life is to feel connected in some way, it's why phones cost what they do. Everybody wants to be heard, no one has anything to say.

'With Marcia I think if we spent some time together she'd open up to me,' I says. Tracey says nothing back, but she's heard me. You lay bait, you wait and most of the time you don't get a bite but that's fine, I've had staff go mental at me, say they'll report me for what I'm asking but in general seems they're advised stuff's best left as is. And she's heard me, 'Siobhan, say hello to your new room mate.' Tracey says to me like it's her idea.

Scene Seven

Tracey   I'm done, it's home time I'm out the door, well I'm on the streets and I'm walking along but I don't wanna go home. See if I'm home then we could have sex and if we do that and nothing happens, just seems more chance that it's me

that can't have them, I don't know why. I'm walking and I'm
on Seven Sisters Road and the first pub I find there's a quiz
on. I so rarely engage it's all . . . Not in the moment, but this.
This is the bit I live for. I'm totally living in this moment. I
should Facebook that I think. Then. The moment's done. I'm
not in the moment am I if I'm Facebooking? But, I just love
quizzes. Mental battles. Felt guilty but with Dad's heart attack,
it was awful I was scared but at least I was feeling something,
being in that moment. He's home now. I just never feel in the
moment. At work I'm counting down the hours. There is
literally no better example of a place where everyone is
winding down the clock. Then at home I'm just thinking, cook
something, eat that thing, watch something a certain length on
the TV. Filling that time before I have to go back to work
which I'm dreading and that's ruining the time I do have.

I could get another job I guess, but that just doesn't seem like
the answer to me, I always feel like there must be an answer,
a better life, like I just need to concentrate hard and I'll find it.
I just want the next bit of my life to happen. But until then
quiz, last question of the round 'What links *Bridget Jones Diary*
and cricket?' and boom, 'Fielding'. I go to the bar in between
rounds and get me another glass of white wine but I can stay
in the moment and we're back and they do this music intro
round, and I'm so in the zone. I'm good on intros. Your first
instinct on something is normally right.

They're gonna announce the winners and I'm waiting and this
woman on the table next to me is vaping, you're not supposed
to inside and it smells like maple syrup or something actually
but to me what it reminds me of is Terry's piss. He drinks too
much, don't know if it's beer or something but our bathroom
just stinks of piss, that stink of maple fucking syrup or
honeycomb or something and I wanna kill her. For a second
I understand how people let their whole life get ruined in one
second. But I know I'm not gonna kill her but I wanna, I
wanna get her drink and pour it all over her cock-coloured
hair. But I breathe and I wait for the answers and I've come
fourth against whole teams. And that's *my* time, that's me

having my time out of work cos now I'm gonna go home, I'm gonna go to bed. I'll wake up tomorrow and have just a bit too long between when you can lie in until and when I actually need to be at work by, and that hour or so in between I'm just gonna spend dreading being back there but when it is my time I'm here, because I'd still rather this to being at home with him.

Scene Eight

Tracey   No I need that Saturday off though it's a wedding. 'We all have to work a number of weekends,' says Paul, like I don't get that. 'Yeah I know we have to work a number of weekends, I've been doing this for . . . What I'm saying is I can't work that Saturday.' 'I'll see what I can do,' he says, like there's a chance that it might not happen. Like I'm gonna miss my own sister's wedding because I've been put down for the wrong shift.

I do get the Saturday swapped and I'm heading to the wedding. I'm travelling on my own, well I'm meeting Terry there because he's spent the Friday night it's some some stupid football thing they do his Sunday League team, event they do. Train on my own is nice actually, Waterloo down to Axminster, it's early but I get myself a cheeky one for the train, one of them gins in a tin, open it and I'm feeling really cheeky. I have that and some Quavers that's my breakfast. Sun's out and lights up the carriage and I'm feeling like this could be just the mini-holiday I need.

Axminster I have to get the bus down from here to where the ceremony is then they're going out on The Cobb for some photos looking out to sea. I've got this bus before and the driver was really mean, hope it's not the same one.

I'm waiting at the bus stop, get my phone out, checking . . . Nothing really, I click on web search to see maybe about buses? But last page I was looking at comes up and it's her, well the news story about her. Mother sentenced after baby remains discovered around family home in seventeen pieces. And I'm reading this, I'm re-reading this and . . . Right yep, that's the bus that gets me to the hotel with enough time to get changed before the wedding. Same bloody driver.

I'm at the stop and I know it's my fault as well and the sun's not out now and I'll have to wait here until . . . Then I'm going to be rushed. I'm thinking about her. Greed I can understand, anger I can understand, stupidity I can understand. I've been greedy, I've been angry, I've been stupid, but that? That I'll never understand.

Scene Nine

Siobhan   Once you're in for life, or a good old stretch, there's no point counting the days or thinking about life out there, you gotta stay in the now and make it as best as bearable as it can be. So that means running things, so that means being the person people come to to get things. There's a risk to this but once you're locked up nearly every hour of the day for longer than you ever saw yourself living that becomes of little fucking bother. Newbies ask, 'How do you get stuff in here?' like it's the postal system out there, like there's one way, like the Royal fucking Mail owning all the stamps, anything postman puts through your letterbox. Well the answer is there's a million fucking ways to get stuff in but the only way you're going to, love, is through me.

Drones, visits, fishing rods made of pieces of your bed and ripped-up sheets to hook up a bag that's been thrown over the walls, mules who pack themselves full of coke and spice then deliberately get themselves locked up for something hoping they don't get it pulled out of them on way in here and screws, screws. With what they're paid and what we can pay, it's no surprise. People ask how do I get stuff in here, well it's all of the above. And I always need more, always need more of all of them. So you keep your eye out, fishing, but not fishing with your home-made rod out your cell window, you see who's got a sign they're weak, if there's the slightest sign they might nibble. I'll reel them in. If you're sad and need a laugh, I can be funny. I can be anything you want me to be, that's how I can get you anything you wanna get.

Scene Ten

Tracey   Running. I'd been talking about starting running for ages then I figured I needed that kick to send, actually get me out there and doing it you know. I sign up for this 10k. I ask Terry if he wants to do it and he kind of goes silent and I'm like 'What?' and he says, he honestly says, 'That's the thing with always being married you end up doing weird stuff together,' and I don't know where to start with that statement. *Always being married*, like there are some people who do it part-time or freelance. And weird stuff, I don't go through his emails or anything but we use the same laptop for stuff and some of his search history like 'my masturbation dot com forward slash kitchen utensils' ain't exactly ordinary and I'm just talking about running around a park to make a few quid for cancer, or against it whatever.

I start training for it and first five minutes of any run from what I can tell it's just your head saying, 'What you doing you crazy lady? Stop this right now, let's go home and we'll have a glass of wine,' but once you're through that it's just the boredom. You're travelling but not actually trying to get anywhere. But I found a way to focus my mind as I beat out this rhythm with my legs, things I'll ask Marcia, the whole conversation, in my head, so when I'm done a run. I'm not knackered, well I am, I'm physically tired but my mind is fresh. I know what I'm gonna say to her. I'm helping her I'm sure.

Running over the heath and I'm by this pond. A posh lady there had a dog off the lead and it's run in the pond cos it's hot I thought but no. It's gone for these little . . . cygnets

I think they're called, little swans, and the mum swan as you can imagine she's gone over and her and some other swans they've dragged this dog and held it under the water. And this posh lady's screaming but they're too far out to get to it in time. And these swans, they've drowned this dog on this beautiful sunny day. Because that's what a mum does.

Scene Eleven

Siobhan Drip. Drip. Drip. That's how you get in. Drop by drop without them seeing. We know. Girls know. For all the bullshit of boys being predatory or whatever. Boys, look on Facebook. The nights you ended up with a girl you thought you had no interest in. Didn't think you were gonna get with, then end of the night you're kissing or in the morning you've woke up with her. Look on Facebook start of the night there'll be a pic of her with a hand on you. Men might think they're the hunter-gatherers but you just make sure the food they need is close enough when they're hungry.

I speak to this male guard, I'm wanting him to bring in some bits for me from a friend, he looks at me like, 'And what do I get in return?' 'This isn't my first rodeo,' I says. 'I never understand that,' he says back, 'I mean most people have not been to a rodeo, why do we use that phrase?' 'OK,' I says, 'this isn't my prom night, I know the score, it's winner stays on and I don't like to lose.' 'Well you do something for me and maybe I can do something for you,' he says like it's his idea. He brings a bag in once a month and I collect the goods so to speak in a store room by the kitchen.

Scene Twelve

Tracey You can't help actually getting to like some of them. This one Siobhan, A19278. You get training and that but it's human beings. Like some of them it's fairly easy not to like on the basis that they're just really horrible, explains why they're in here. But you get some and they're just funny. Siobhan's always coming out with stuff like, 'If you wanna knock off early I can lock up.' I suppose if anyone was half decent at being a criminal they wouldn't be in here would they? There's nothing like enough police to deal with even the obvious crime we're facing. No it's the super-flash or super-thick end up in here.

Like being a doctor and friends all telling you their medical stuff, once people hear you work in prisons they'll tell you all about any crimes happen to them and you can be like, 'I'm just having a wine can we not . . . ?' but even those stories can be quite funny. Terry's friend tells me he gets home and the place has been burgled, they've kicked the door until the wood's broken and snapped. Hours later the police arrive and they look at it and they go, 'They know what they're doing these burglars,' Like Mori-bloody-arty has masterminded this, like a team of super-criminals have put their minds together and decided to kick a piece of wood until it breaks. That's what I mean, police are too busy to catch even door-kickers so if you end up in here you've done something very wrong and by wrong I mean dumb.

You've either walked into an electrical store and stolen a video camera which is both turned on and pointing at your face while it's relayed to all the TVs in that same shop, don't laugh someone actually did that, their own friends grassed 'em up probably thinking they were safer off inside than on their own. Or you've gone too flash, you've been driving around in another brand-new car and you get noticed. If I was . . . not that we would but if as a married couple you were growing weed say? Set up a small fake walled-off bit half your cellar, nothing too big. And you make sure you've got something, workwise, part-time in a beauty salon or something and he has similar, drives a . . . minicab. No one knows what hours either of you are supposed to be working, earning, so if you're on holiday a few times a year nobody's gonna know are they? That's how I'd do it, but I never would, even slightly outside the line. It's just not worth the risk, end up in here. But they are funny some of them. 'I can lock up.'

Scene Thirteen

Siobhan   Games. You can do a few activities in here. Like PE. Think that was the only lesson I liked at school. The other girls would always be looking for ways out of it, getting notes from their mum, bitching about it to the other girls. Moaning about the teachers, calling the women ones dykes and the blokes pervs but . . . I liked it. It's a different type of challenge isn't it? People think it's just a physical thing but it's not, most of it's up here. You win most things like that up here. Get the words right, get the right look in your eye and make sure whoever you're up against sees it, knows not to mess with ya.

See in here's a sport same as netball or hockey. You just let people know what'll happen if they try to compete with you. Life's all games that we play with each other, some in our heads and some not. I could tell you about my ex, that he deserved it, what he's done to me, what he'd been doing to me for years. That the fact that I'd got away from that didn't actually make it any easier, that I couldn't, didn't want to move on. That all this is worth it to not have him on the planet. Like I'm the real sufferer from all this. I could make you feel sorry for me, make you laugh, make you like me. But that would be just as much a game as what I'm doing now, making you think I'm tough, that I'm OK in here that I'm not scared. So I'm not gonna lie to you. Am I?

Scene Fourteen

Tracey   I made a mistake. It's the dumbest, I can't believe I did but since Dad's heart attack I've been telling him he should have check-ups at doctor's but he says there is no point going to the doctor. He says, 'If you're going to the doctor you can't be that ill because if you were you should be going to hospital and if that's the case you're dead.' Hard to believe Mum left him eh? With that sort of flawless logic. I left him to it, he'd been on the mend it seemed, then he took a turn for the worse, so I was really . . . I didn't know what to do. I could just hear he was . . . This was not getting better so I . . . I did a stupid thing a tiny thing. I brought my phone with me on shift. On silent. On vibrate. I just wanted . . . I didn't want it to be a whole shift before I found out that he'd . . . If he . . . Got worse. So I've my phone on me and it's on silent and nobody is gonna see it.

Siobhan   I sit, I wait, I observe. Everything in here, everything is a little everything. A butterfly flutters its wings and there's an earthquake other side of the world. A phone vibrates in a pocket of an officer and I'm remembering something Marcia told me. 'Tracey, talk to me.'

Tracey   Siobhan says she wants to tell me something. She knows I find Marcia a . . . I don't know, like a snowball question at the end of the competition. I just wanna get inside that head. So I ask Siobhan if we can speak inside her cell. She doesn't want to.

Siobhan   I do want to. I say, 'Oh I spend enough time in there can't we . . . ' But we need some alone time. And I'm telling her all the things Marcia's said to me, what she's said to the other girls but I'm watching her leg, just waiting for that leg to . . . (*Vibration movement with hand.*) And it does. It goes.

Tracey   And I do this stupid thing. I make a mistake, but . . . But this'll be fine because, I know you can't trust any of them. I don't trust any of them, as a rule, that's a good rule but . . . Well it might be my dad and I get my phone out and it's . . . It's Papa bloody John's I ordered a pizza off them at some point and now they just send a text every, I don't know with some nonsense and Siobhan sees me look at the phone and so I explain, I don't need to explain myself, not to her but I do explain my dad isn't well and . . .

Siobhan   And I laugh about Papa John because I tell her my dad's called John and some story about how he cooked a pizza for me when I was a little girl but he left the plastic polystyrene thing to keep its shape, that supermarket thing on the bottom how he's left that on in the oven and we've eaten it or tried to eat it but it tastes like licking an ash tray. Then I go a bit quiet and mention my dad's not very well either. 'Could I send a text message?'

Tracey   And I pass her the phone.

We see **Siobhan** *send a text message and hear it received.*

Scene Fifteen

Tracey   Couldn't sleep that night, the next morning I decide I've got to go to Paul, my boss, I'll tell him how it happened. Leap of faith. I made a mistake but I'm a good person. But he's . . . I find him and there's two in there with him having a coffee. And George who's there, likes to talk, loves to talk he's going on about does anyone know an electrician? 'The electrics in my house they're all back to front I reckon, see you put the dryer on, to dry your clothes and our TV it starts to flicker, not sure if our whole street has it but I want someone to take a look. See it's that, and my Mary when she puts her electric blanket on at night it changes the channel on the Sky Box. Must be the electric blanket cos only thing we have on once we go to bed. It flicks the Sky Box over to those porno freeview channels. Must be Mary's blanket as I don't watch that filth and my thirteen-year-old boy swears me it's not him.'

Eyebrows are raised at this and nobody says anything, then my boss Paul says, 'I could take a look if you like, I always thought of myself as a bit of a sparky.' But George is dubious, 'Wanting to be something don't make you it, does it. If a homeless man gives a blowjob to a paedophile that doesn't make him a child.'

Certainly has a way with words, George, but it makes me
realise, however good a person I think I am, I've still done this
thing. I can't tell anyone. I'm gonna get serious with the
running, get super-fit I reckon.

Scene Sixteen

Siobhan   Was she working for me? Tracey? Well, I don't
think that's really the point is it? I'm not sure why anyone
ever looked for various ways to skin a cat. I know there's that
stupid expression but . . . People from different places do things
differently don't they, fast or slow. You see a new officer start
and someone will be on them like friendly, 'Where are you
from? I know around there, which bit? That where your family
are from? Yeah. Bring this in for me. I've got friends around
there and it would be a shame if your family were burnt to
death in the night in a gas explosion.'

That's not me see, there's no rush, no need to scare people,
you gotta think long-term, bring them under your wing, in
time. You see, I know how to live, in here. You ever tried to live
with absolutely nothing holding your day together? You tried
it? You don't even know what I mean, how could you? I tell
you it's a lot fucking easier in here than trying to do that.
Unemployed and sober, sleeping at night but there's no reason
to go to sleep, you're not tired and there's nothing in the
morning to get up for. In here, they get you up, better than
out there. Having a day, nothing breaking one bit and the
next. Like a holiday but it ain't like a holiday. A holiday ain't a
holiday if you've nothing to go back to. Work is structure,
heroin gives structure, in here there's structure. None are
great but . . . But hell of a lot better than having nothing in
front of you.

Scene Seventeen

Tracey   Search of the wing and I'm doing a cell. This is mental but the aim is to find stuff, phones, drugs, stuff they're not allowed, but also we don't wanna find too much. Cos if we find too much we get fined, as a business the prison does, more than five phones found and there's a fine so you wanna do your job as best you can but there's also that subtle pressure to not do it too well. And we've found five that day and I look in this cell and I could turn the whole place over, there's some photos stuck to the wall with something, I have a quick look behind them to see any baggies of spice or whatever, they love that stuff, used to be able to just buy it off stalls in Camden, illegal now but doesn't show up on drug tests. There's nothing behind the pictures which are stuck to the wall with Sellotape. Nothing in the cell looks like a phone or charger and I won't be thanked if I do find one so I'm out. I check Siobhan's cell last, feel what could be that roll of Sellotape under the bed but guess they're using it to put their pictures on the walls, no drugs, no phones so we're on five and that's OK.

It'll sound stupid but the amount they're paying for phones makes me think I might go pay-as-you-go, like a teenager, 'Call me back I've no credit,' might stop me being on it the whole time though, any wait of more than ten seconds I'm online checking. Might go pay-as-you-go.

Scene Eighteen

Siobhan   She'll have got a response to that text now I don't know what that will have been, I can't put words in other people's mouths or inboxes, but what I imagine it will have said is, 'You're one of us now.' See I can stay friendly with her, but she knows now I've sent information out to someone, something that however indirectly, however coded, could end up affecting life in here, put the other officers in danger, in any way. Well, she knows that line's been crossed. And once you've crossed that line just a step, half-step, that's all it needs because who you going to go to? And it'll start out nice, start out just seeming totally harmless 'Don't worry about it, just chuck a new mobile to so-and-so and we'll forget all about this and five hundred quid for your trouble.' But nothing ever stops there. Because once you've done that for us and we're friends we can stay friends it doesn't have to change, the dynamic never has to change. Unless you make it, unless you try and stop this and then it can get very nasty indeed.

And it's the smallest things, the smallest detail. Nothing nasty, nobody gonna get hurt, just if you're doing a search let me know and do mine last. It's not a dodgy thing I just hate surprises and we're mates now, we don't need to surprise each other, don't need secrets between us now, do we? I'm the one keeping you in the know letting you know about your favourite baby-killer. I'm not asking you to change from what you're supposed to do, meant to do on your routine but, little things don't need to be made a big deal out of, do they? Harmless things?

Scene Nineteen

Tracey   I'm walking these streets, but I'll never be free. My flat's around the back of work opposite the Odeon. I remember when we moved in so full of hope, extra bedroom we'd make a nursery, just Terry's weight machine there now and drying horse for washing. They had flats there for staff, right by work, but the layout, it's exactly like the prison. That's why I'm the only one from there lives here now, that and wages mean it's hard to not live a lot further out. Terry earns, he does OK. See when I was starting, loads of them used to try to get in your head, try to find out things about you, surprise you, mention someone you knew that you'd never mentioned to them but that never got to me. But one thing still stands out. It was a woman what weren't trying that, just as she was going back in her cell she sees me behind her and over her shoulder sort of mumbled to herself, 'Who protects those that protect us?'

It ain't a vocation, a friend and me were both temping then this came up. She put it best, we work to keep ourselves alive but each day kills us more inside. I see a woman, every day, locked up, locked up cos what she did meant her child died. But she's free, she's free cos she in her head for whatever reason thinks only the bad is now gone. But you can't only remove what is bad, you can't only have the answers to questions that'll come up in this week's quiz in your head. You can't choose your memories and I spend more time in prison than most of them. But what's the answer? To this I don't know the answer.

Scene Twenty

Siobhan   As they'll have opened that cell, I know what they'll have seen. Not a glamorous death, not that there is such a thing. But not a poetic one we picture with a what-you-call-that-thing? Something you could hook over in the ceiling, a hook, that's the word, something giving you height and a rope and a chair to kick away and give you the height you need. No, they'll have seen the result of the truly desperate. (*She demonstrates her description.*) Once the determination is to die, you don't need your legs to dangle, so a home-made material with which to garrote yourself tethered around something away enough from the ground that if you fall, that small drop, like you're moving to sit on your arse but you won't get that far, it won't snap your neck but will let the life slowly strangle from you and if that's your aim and it will have been. To say goodbye. That's what they'll have seen and I know that not because I was there. You believe me don't you? I wouldn't lie to you would I?

Scene Twenty-One

Tracey   To be honest with you I don't really believe much in reform. I'm not sure people really change. You ever bought a packet of seeds? I did, I thought I'd take up a bit of gardening so I've bought this pack and I think it'll be like loads, like a bag of skittles or whatever but smaller, but no. No I open this pack and I think I've been conned, think it's a dodgy pack because there's like four in there. So I open the other pack I bought which is from another brand and it's the same, like four seeds, that's how it happens. That's all you get and you have to hope it grows. So I plant them, I've put them in this little pot in the garden and I look out and birds just come, it's almost straight away they come and they just eat them all. They're not evil or anything they're just . . . birds. And I just want to protect them. I don't want to try and make birds not eat seeds, I just want to protect the flowers.

I had this chat with Marcia, the day after a long run. I really felt I'd got an answer. Like I'd won the tie-breaker. Like all the Googling, thinking about her, obsessing had been worth it. That I could move on now. Because there's this change in her eyes as I'm talking to her about her boyfriend, him that did all that, cutting out the evil, then disappearing. I feel like talking about him the penny's dropped and she's seen what she's done, what she's been part of. That there's no God and if there was he wouldn't want anyone to do that kind of thing but mainly that there just isn't one. That there's just here, what's happening to you now. And even after for her it's not gonna be the kind of thing you can walk away from. Ever. It's not, 'Well I did a load of shoplifting when I was younger but I've got myself together now.' That is always there.

And I'm glad I see this breakthrough. I know that's not my job, I know there's people whose job it is to try to do this with her but I don't know, ever since seeing that case I just knew I could . . . Once I could make her realise this I could. I'd be ready to be a mum and maybe that's what's been holding stuff back. But now I don't know if she ever was ready to face it.

Before that we'd been laughing. She'd always be smiling, thinly hiding the fear normally but this was the only time she laughed. We have this daft woman come in try to teach them art. She's called Grace, she speaks like this, honestly, 'So what I think, what I truly believe is that it doesn't matter what anyone's done, that's behind them I can't do anything with that. But what I can do and what's important is not what people have done but the art they can create. That's what really makes me happy. That and drinking cider at the horse show.'

And her and Siobhan have done this class and they're making these . . . Honestly it's like what you'd do with toddlers, it's like sticking pasta to paper type thing, except they're using Sellotape with these. Grace the teacher at the end is counting her materials back in and she's like, 'I'll have to get more tape, they used a lot, I thought I'd brought in six.' I look for an empty used-up roll, 'I must have miscounted,' she says.

Scene Twenty-Two

Tracey   Back at the wedding. It's summer. It's just really nice here, by the sea, Devon, Dorset, border I think. People say hello to each other, like random people walking along, can see why sis wanted to get married here now . . . I used the loo at this little house they're renting out, my sister's staying there and Pete her boyfriend . . . husband, I'll have to get used to that as of today. Anyway in the loo there's one of them hundred ways to relax books. A hundred is a lot isn't it? How'd you find the time? Stresses me out just thinking about it. I don't look at it. What you can't see can't hurt you.

I have a little cry. I'm not sad it's just that. It's when you've been looking forward to something for so long then when it happens as great as it is you're worried that by worrying you're ruining the memory of the thing you'd been looking forward to so much. I'm nervous going back to work, I could try again to talk to Paul, my boss, explain. But then he has to send it up the chain of command and . . . It's not just the job, George's stories about colleagues he's seen become inmates, and I just can't do that. Did you ever do something when you were a kid and you think it's really bad and you're quiet about it then eventually you tell your dad and he lets you know it's nothing to worry about and gives you a kiss and everything's OK. And Dad's here at the wedding but he's not OK either, he's pretending to be though. And I'm an adult and I just have to deal with this one myself.

I don't belong here. I stand out. In London, I like that, nobody stands out, way too many of us to notice who should or shouldn't be there. Things stand out down here, stand out as clearly as the Cobb does heading out into the sea cos the biggest crimes going on are, well local paper says the council are considering making feeding seagulls an offence and there's an actual sign saying 'This car park is annually checked so it's safer for you and your vehicle.' Annually. Here things stand out but in London there are much worse things happening, worse things than my little mistake. I'll be fine won't I?

Scene Twenty-Three

Siobhan   I . . . for all the reasons I have for doing things, for any agenda. I've still done them haven't I? I spoke to Marcia and this wasn't to get anything, this wasn't for ammunition what might be useful because she started talking and I realised something. I saw something in her. Me, well me at a time and that just . . . that just shouldn't be in someone. And what you see is men, well, a particular type of man, a controlling man. A man who makes you feel, makes you think that without him there'd be . . . nothing. And at times that can feel so amazing can feel so good when they're making plans, telling you their plans, telling you you're the centre of those plans. But then when you don't fit into that, when you seem to question even in the slightest way. Well, that's when you see the other side of it. And you don't wanna see the other side of it. Believe me you don't. So you let them do . . . you let them do anything, crazy as stupid as they might sound, seem. I can see it in her, that's still there, that she just believed this man and she tells me what happened and that she wasn't even there she certainly had no part of it but she trusted him, still trusts him. And there is that point. That point of no fucking return where you think without him you're nothing so if he's gone. Well why not, just let whatever happens happen, let it all come piling down because without him . . . And I see that in her and it's still there. And I know that it's never going to go away. And I know there's only one way I can get that out of her. She had nothing to do with it, the baby, any of it. And I knew there was only one way I could sort this for her.

Scene Twenty-Four

Tracey   We had someone come in, give us training, trust-building exercises. Confidence, it's supposed to give us in ourselves, in each other. Team-building thing. Load of nonsense in the main but some of it stuck with me so I guess . . . The fella who runs it, he's wearing this Hawaiian shirt, short sleeves, bright colours, lairy I'd call it. He seems a right dick, he starts the session says we should all share something about ourselves and he starts and I'm thinking, 'Everybody wants to be heard, no one has anything to say,' and he's telling us to do stuff, walk around close our eyes and I'm just staring at him. Few of the others notice this and laugh but I'm not trying to make any specific point, I'm staring at him and the others just get on with it, they're smiling and I can tell they're probably thinking same thing as me but they're playing the game. Even Paul, who's in charge of the day our end, he sees I'm giving this guy daggers and just laughs, to himself, quietly.

Anyway the fella running this, Mr Hawaiian-shirt fella he doesn't seem to have clocked these looks from me, but as we get to the end, the last exercise, he says we're gonna do that day he singles me out, he says we need a brave individual for

this last exercise and he picks me out, calls me over and . . .
And he lines everyone up facing each other tells everyone to
get in a pair with someone roughly their height and then tells
'em to put their arms out, like this.

She holds her arms out at shoulder height in front of herself.

And he tells me to climb up on the table. Our fella Paul looks
a bit nervous on this, like health and safety but Mr Hawaiian
shirt holds up a hand to say like it's all fine. And everyone's got
their arms out in front of them like but interlinked, not touching
but each with one arm between the two of the person they're
facing and he tells me to take a leap, of faith. Just jump into
the arms of my team. That they'll carry me. They'll catch me.
Even if I don't think they can even if *they* don't think they can
take this leap. And I'm looking at this prick and the rest of the
team are looking at him the same. So he gets up on the table
and I can see the group now, they're relaxing their arms, they
had 'em tense when it was me up there but with him I can see
they're not trying and I'm thinking, this is it, this is gonna be
fucking hilarious, this guy's about to jump, fall through their
arms and disable himself on the floor.

But he jumps and he lands and it's safe, he's the only one not
surprised, no one was trying to catch him but the group just
holding their arms out like that is enough. So now I'm up on
the table and I jump and again they catch me, it's no burden,
no effort, I'm held, I'm supported, I'm weightless, well near
enough weightless cos the team they can take it, it's nothing.
So then I swap with the next person gonna jump and my arms
are in this . . . safety net, I guess you'd call it, this thing we've
built between us and my colleague jumps and we catch him,
I catch him and he's a big fella, must weigh double, well not
double me, I wish, but he's big.

That's the thing see, see things which don't seem very strong
on their own they can be . . . When combined when forged
together . . . Like Sellotape. Thing with a roll of tape tricky to
work out where they begin cos they're circular. But once you've
started they unravel. Seem weak but. Used the right way . . .

See, you can tear tape into little pieces and wrap your Christmas presents and stuff but if you let it unravel, unravel and wrap it around itself, tighter, thicker, stronger. You keep wrapping that around itself and like us that day it can bear weight. It can become circular again like the roll it was on but stronger this time, worse this time, because now you can wrap it around a neck. And this DIY noose can suddenly become very useful inside, if you're someone inside and think this is your only way out. So that Christmas Day when they found Marcia, well, that roll of tape proved very significant indeed. What's a four-letter word which can also be a sentence? Life. Siobhan looks at me and smiles and just whispers in my ear, 'You're one of us now.'

This is how it ends.

Finish.

Bloomsbury Methuen Drama Modern Plays
include work by

Bola Agbaje	Robert Holman
Edward Albee	Caroline Horton
Davey Anderson	Terry Johnson
Jean Anouilh	Sarah Kane
John Arden	Barrie Keeffe
Peter Barnes	Doug Lucie
Sebastian Barry	Anders Lustgarten
Alistair Beaton	David Mamet
Brendan Behan	Patrick Marber
Edward Bond	Martin McDonagh
William Boyd	Arthur Miller
Bertolt Brecht	D. C. Moore
Howard Brenton	Tom Murphy
Amelia Bullmore	Phyllis Nagy
Anthony Burgess	Anthony Neilson
Leo Butler	Peter Nichols
Jim Cartwright	Joe Orton
Lolita Chakrabarti	Joe Penhall
Caryl Churchill	Luigi Pirandello
Lucinda Coxon	Stephen Poliakoff
Curious Directive	Lucy Prebble
Nick Darke	Peter Quilter
Shelagh Delaney	Mark Ravenhill
Ishy Din	Philip Ridley
Claire Dowie	Willy Russell
David Edgar	Jean-Paul Sartre
David Eldridge	Sam Shepard
Dario Fo	Martin Sherman
Michael Frayn	Wole Soyinka
John Godber	Simon Stephens
Paul Godfrey	Peter Straughan
James Graham	Kate Tempest
David Greig	Theatre Workshop
John Guare	Judy Upton
Mark Haddon	Timberlake Wertenbaker
Peter Handke	Roy Williams
David Harrower	Snoo Wilson
Jonathan Harvey	Frances Ya-Chu Cowhig
Iain Heggie	Benjamin Zephaniah

Bloomsbury Methuen Drama Contemporary Dramatists

include

John Arden (two volumes)
Arden & D'Arcy
Peter Barnes (three volumes)
Sebastian Barry
Mike Bartlett
Dermot Bolger
Edward Bond (eight volumes)
Howard Brenton (two volumes)
Leo Butler
Richard Cameron
Jim Cartwright
Caryl Churchill (two volumes)
Complicite
Sarah Daniels (two volumes)
Nick Darke
David Edgar (three volumes)
David Eldridge (two volumes)
Ben Elton
Per Olov Enquist
Dario Fo (two volumes)
Michael Frayn (four volumes)
John Godber (four volumes)
Paul Godfrey
James Graham
David Greig
John Guare
Lee Hall (two volumes)
Katori Hall
Peter Handke
Jonathan Harvey (two volumes)
Iain Heggie
Israel Horovitz
Declan Hughes
Terry Johnson (three volumes)
Sarah Kane
Barrie Keeffe
Bernard-Marie Koltès (two volumes)
Franz Xaver Kroetz
Kwame Kwei-Armah
David Lan
Bryony Lavery
Deborah Levy
Doug Lucie

David Mamet (four volumes)
Patrick Marber
Martin McDonagh
Duncan McLean
David Mercer (two volumes)
Anthony Minghella (two volumes)
Tom Murphy (six volumes)
Phyllis Nagy
Anthony Neilson (two volumes)
Peter Nichol (two volumes)
Philip Osment
Gary Owen
Louise Page
Stewart Parker (two volumes)
Joe Penhall (two volumes)
Stephen Poliakoff (three volumes)
David Rabe (two volumes)
Mark Ravenhill (three volumes)
Christina Reid
Philip Ridley (two volumes)
Willy Russell
Eric-Emmanuel Schmitt
Ntozake Shange
Sam Shepard (two volumes)
Martin Sherman (two volumes)
Christopher Shinn
Joshua Sobel
Wole Soyinka (two volumes)
Simon Stephens (three volumes)
Shelagh Stephenson
David Storey (three volumes)
C. P. Taylor
Sue Townsend
Judy Upton
Michel Vinaver (two volumes)
Arnold Wesker (two volumes)
Peter Whelan
Michael Wilcox
Roy Williams (four volumes)
David Williamson
Snoo Wilson (two volumes)
David Wood (two volumes)
Victoria Wood

Bloomsbury Methuen Drama Student Editions

Jean Anouilh *Antigone* • John Arden *Serjeant Musgrave's Dance* • Alan Ayckbourn *Confusions* • Aphra Behn *The Rover* • Edward Bond *Lear* • *Saved* • Bertolt Brecht *The Caucasian Chalk Circle* • *Fear and Misery in the Third Reich* • *The Good Person of Szechwan* • *Life of Galileo* • *Mother Courage and Her Children* • *The Resistible Rise of Arturo Ui* • *The Threepenny Opera* • Anton Chekhov *The Cherry Orchard* • *The Seagull* • *Three Sisters* • *Uncle Vanya* • Caryl Churchill *Serious Money* • *Top Girls* • Shelagh Delaney *A Taste of Honey* • Euripides *Elektra* • *Medea* • Dario Fo *Accidental Death of an Anarchist* • Michael Frayn *Copenhagen* • John Galsworthy *Strife* • Nikolai Gogol *The Government Inspector* • Carlo Goldoni *A Servant to Two Masters* • Lorraine Hansberry *A Raisin in the Sun* • Robert Holman *Across Oka* • Henrik Ibsen *A Doll's House* • *Ghosts* • *Hedda Gabler* • Sarah Kane *4.48 Psychosis* • *Blasted* • Charlotte Keatley *My Mother Said I Never Should* • Bernard Kops *Dreams of Anne Frank* • Federico García Lorca *Blood Wedding* • *Doña Rosita the Spinster* (bilingual edition) • *The House of Bernarda Alba* (bilingual edition) • *Yerma* (bilingual edition) • David Mamet *Glengarry Glen Ross* • *Oleanna* • Patrick Marber *Closer* • John Marston *The Malcontent* • Martin McDonagh *The Lieutenant of Inishmore* • *The Lonesome West* • *The Beauty Queen of Leenane* • Arthur Miller *All My Sons* • *The Crucible* • *A View from the Bridge* • *Death of a Salesman* • *The Price* • *After the Fall* • *The Last Yankee* • *A Memory of Two Mondays* • *Broken Glass* • Joe Orton *Loot* • Joe Penhall *Blue/Orange* • Luigi Pirandello *Six Characters in Search of an Author* • Lucy Prebble *Enron* • Mark Ravenhill *Shopping and F***ing* • Willy Russell *Blood Brothers* • *Educating Rita* • Sophocles *Antigone* • *Oedipus the King* • Wole Soyinka *Death and the King's Horseman* • Shelagh Stephenson *The Memory of Water* • August Strindberg *Miss Julie* • J. M. Synge *The Playboy of the Western World* • Theatre Workshop *Oh What a Lovely War* • Frank Wedekind *Spring Awakening* • Timberlake Wertenbaker *Our Country's Good* • Arnold Wesker *The Merchant* • Oscar Wilde *The Importance of Being Earnest* • Tennessee Williams *A Streetcar Named Desire* • *The Glass Menagerie* • *Cat on a Hot Tin Roof* • *Sweet Bird of Youth*